GERMAN PIONEERS

IN EARLY CALIFORNIA

ERWIN G. GUDDE'S HISTORY

EDITED BY DON HEINRICH TOLZMANN

I0115670

HERITAGE BOOKS
2007

HERITAGE BOOKS
AN IMPRINT OF HERITAGE BOOKS, INC.

Books, CDs, and more—Worldwide

For our listing of thousands of titles see our website
at
www.HeritageBooks.com

Published 2007 by
HERITAGE BOOKS, INC.
Publishing Division
65 East Main Street
Westminster, Maryland 21157-5026

Originally published 1927
Copyright © 2007 Don Heinrich Tolzmann

International Standard Book Number: 978-0-7884-1822-8

TABLE OF CONTENTS

EDITOR'S INTRODUCTION

California has more German-Americans than any state in the Union, according to the 1990 U.S. Census.[1] Close to five million Californians claim German heritage. This translates into roughly 17% of the state's population.

Since the 18th century, close to a hundred German-American newspapers have been published in California, which provide a rich storehouse of information on the history of German immigration, settlement and influences on the state.[2]

Unfortunately, no general up-to-date history of California's German heritage is available, although there are a number of histories on the German element in various parts of the state.[3]

The purpose of this work is to contribute to an understanding of California's German heritage by making a work, originally published in 1927, again available and accessible to all those interested in the topic.[4]

Although published some time ago, this work has never been replaced, and it, therefore, seemed a work worthy of re-publication at this time. To facilitate access to the work an index of names has been added.

Don Heinrich Tolzmann
University of Cincinnati

Notes

1. See Don Heinrich Tolzmann, *The German-American Experience.* (Amherst, New York: Humanity Books, 2000), p. 454.

2. For a list of California's German-American newspapers, see Karl J. R. Arndt, *The German-Language Press of the Americas.* (MŸnchen: K.G. Saur, 1976), vol. 1, pp. 21-34.

3. See Don Heinrich Tolzmann, *Catalog of the German-Americana Collection, University of Cincinnati.* (MŸnchen: K.G. Saur, 1990), vol. 1, pp. 331-34. Also, see Don Heinrich Tolzmann, *German-Americana: A Bibliography.* (Metuchen, New Jersey: The Scarecrow Press, 1975), pp. 28-29.

4. This work was originally published as: Erwin G. Gudde, *German Pioneers in Early California.* (Hoboken, NJ: The Concord Society, 1927).

31

Pioneer Monument at Donner Lake

PREFACE

The following account of the part played by Germans and German-Americans in the pioneer stages of the history of California is the forerunner of a more extensive work on the German element in California. Although this presentation is based on reliable historical sources, I have refrained from quoting references or adding a bibliography. Since it was written, not for the professional historian, but for a wide circle of readers, I deemed it advisable not to burden it with any critical apparatus.

Of the many general histories of California, none has been more useful for my purpose then Hubert H. Bancroft's *History of California*. This, as well as the other works of this historian, form a most valuable source of information. Of some assistance were May Wheeler's *John A. Sutter, a California Pioneer*, Clarence Du Four's *John A. Sutter, his Career in California before the American Conquest*, and especially George Hammond's *German Interest in California before 1850*,—all dissertations written in Professor Herbert Bolton's seminar, where the present writer's interest in Western American history was also first aroused. The abundance of printed and written material on the history of California contained in the Bancroft Library of the University of California has yielded a rich harvest of information on my particular subject, only a small part of which I have been able to work into this essay. To Mr. Joseph Hill of the Bancroft Library and to Miss Leona Fassett I am indebted for kind assistance. The illustrations of Sutter's Fort and of Stockton were taken from Coy's Pictorial History of California with the permission of the Extension Division of the University of California.

Berkeley, July 1927.   E. G. G.

Father Kino and the German Jesuits

The early history of California is identical with the history of the northward expansion of New Spain, the present-day Mexico. Beginning with the latter part of the seventeenth century, the missions of the northern frontier were mainly in the hands of German Jesuits. One of them, Eusebius Franciscus Kino, is the most outstanding figure of the first period of California history.

Father Kino was born in 1644 in Hala, a little town in the valley of Nonsburg in Tyrol. After graduating from the Latin school of his native town, he studied at the Universities of Ingolstadt and Freiburg. In 1665 he entered the Province of Upper Germany of the Society of Jesu and became a teacher of grammar. His knowledge of the mathematical sciences earned him the honorable call to a professorship at the University of Ingolstadt. Kino, however, preferred to devote his life to missionary work among the heathens, and with a great number of other Jesuits from Central Europe he set sail for Mexico in 1681.

From the very outset Father Kino showed an enthusiastic interest in the spiritual conquest of California. In 1683 he established the first mission in Lower California. Although the attempt came finally to naught because of Spanish mismanagement, Kino's interest in the project remained, and it was due mainly to his efforts that ten years later his friend and disciple, Juan Salvatierra, carried the idea to a successful conclusion.

Kino himself had found a fruitful field for his endeavors in Pimeria Alta. In the region of the Gila and Colorado rivers on both sides of the present U. S.-Mexican boundary, the great missionary labored untiringly until his death in 1711, acquiring great fame as missionary, educator, rancher, scientist, and explorer. His magnetic personality, his tact and gentleness in treating the natives, his robust health, his vast knowledge, were the reasons for his great success. Of special interest for the history of California are Kino's activities as explorer. At least once a year he would set out on horseback, often accompanied only by a few of his faithful Indians. His chief effort was directed toward the discovery of a land route between Sonora and California. He was probably never quite convinced of the current theory that Lower California was an island, and in 1702 he proved to his satisfaction that California was a part of the mainland and drafted the first correct map of this region. In his reports Kino continually urged the northward extension of the frontier, and for the next century the Spanish expansion in California and Arizona followed essentially the proposals laid down by Father Kino. He was, according to Gilmary Shea, "the greatest missionary who labored in North America."

Kino's Map of California

Other German Jesuits continued the work of their great countryman. Johann G r a s h o f f e r. Philipp Segesser and Kaspar Steiger established the first permanent missions and settlements within the present limits of the United States, while Jacob Sedelmair and Ignatz Keller gained recognition as explorers. A presentation of their labors belongs, however, to the history of Arizona. In Lower California the missions were also mainly in the hands of Germans. In 1760 they numbered eight among the sixteen Jesuits who had charge of the settlements in that part of the Spanish empire.

Of special historical interest are the writings of these Jesuits. The *memoirs* of Kino and Sedelmair, the former recently edited and published by Professor Herbert Bolton, are of great importance for the early history of Arizona, while Jacob Baegert's *Nachrichten von der amerikanischen Halbinsel California* was the first authentic account of California. The importance of this work is witnessed by the fact that the Smithsonian Institute republished a part of it some hundred years later. One of the most valuable sources of Western American history is Stoecklein's *Der Neuwe Welt-Bott*, a collection of letters and reports written by the Jesuits to relatives and superiors in the old country.

In 1767 the great work of the Jesuits came to an abrupt end. After the prohibition of the order its members were disgracefully deported, and the Franciscans were entrusted with the further colonization of California. The three or four decades following the expulsion of the Jesuits constitute the only period of California history in which the German element did not play a prominent role, although we find some Germans among the early settlers, the Franciscan friars, and the employees of the merchant adventurers and the Russian American Company.

Explorers, Traders and Trappers

It was due mainly to the reports of German scientists and explorers that at the beginning of the nineteenth century California ceased to be a mere geographical expression and became known to the world as a country whose yet undeveloped resources promised a great future. The Russians coming from the North were the first to dispute the claims of the Spaniards, who by the end of the eighteenth century had pushed their frontier beyond the Bay of San Francisco. In the ensuing decades England, France, and Prussia became interested in the acquisition of California. Yet, after the Louisiana purchase in 1803, it seemed a foregone conclusion that this beautiful country would finally become a part of the great American republic, and no less a personality than Goethe prophesied in 1827 the conquest of the Pacific coast by the United States within 30 or 40 years.

The first two reports on Upper California, i. e. the present state, were those by Robert Shaler and Alexander von Humboldt, who both visited Mexico in 1804. Shaler's report, though suggesting the annexation of California to the United States, was of little consequence for the future history of the country; but Humboldt's *Political Essay of the Kingdom of New Spain*, published in German, English, French, and Spanish, created a world-wide interest. The great German scientist never set his foot on California soil, but compiled his chapter on the *Intendancy of New California* from the archives of Mexico

City and from the reports of persons acquainted with California. Nevertheless it was the first reliable account of the conditions of California, and other writers borrowed freely from it. Alexander von Humboldt has been honored more than any other man in the naming of the Pacific Southwest and in numerous public institutions.

The first German explorer to give to the world a description of California based on actual observation was G. H. von Langsdorff. Originally a scientific member of the Krusenstern expedition to the North Pacific, in 1806 Langsdorff went south with the Russian commissioner, Rezanof, and stayed several months in California. Langsdorff's narrative, published in 1813 in German and English, was "the most detailed account of the country and its population that had yet been given to the world," as one historian remarks.

Of equal importance was the visit of the *Rurik* in 1816. Although a Russian enterprise, the commander, Otto von Kotzebue, a son of the famous playwright, and the members of the scientific staff were Germans. The most interesting personality on the *Rurik* was Adelbert von Chamisso, known all over the world for his marvelous story of Peter Schlemihl, the man without a shadow. Chamisso's observations are still more detailed and more valuable than those of Langsdorff. He gives excellent descriptions of the flora and fauna of the region around San Francisco Bay, of the Indian tribes, and of the general political and social conditions. To Chamisso belongs also the honor of having discovered, classified, and baptized California's beautiful state-flower, the Golden Poppy. He named it *Eschscholtzia Californica* after his friend Dr. I. Eschscholtz, the ship's doctor. Besides the works of Kotzebue and Chamisso, the artist of the expedition, Ludwig Choris, likewise a German, published an illustrated account of the voyage. His book contains probably the first pictures of California ever printed, among them an image of the symbol in California's coat of arms, the Grizzly Bear.

In 1824 Kotzebue paid another visit to San Francisco while in command of a Russian expedition around the world. His staff again consisted exclusively of Germans. The bay of San Francisco was thoroughly explored and much new information added to the knowledge of the geography and zoology of California.

There were many other Germans in the Russian service connected with the history of California. The two Alaskan governors of that period, Hegemeister and

Wrangel, paid frequent visits to the country, and the vessel which in 1812 brought the Russians to California for the settlement of Fort Ross was in command of Christian Beusemann, a Prussian. M. von Schmidt, for many years the governor of Fort Ross, brought the establishment to an admirable degree of perfection, and, to the amazement of the natives, erected a wind-mill, the first on the Pacific Coast.

The most important California merchant of the twenties and thirties was Heinrich Virmond, a Rhinelander by birth, with offices in Mexico City and Acapulco. He was in high favor with the Mexican government and, till his early death, practically monopolized the legitimate trade of California. With his fleet of merchantmen he instituted the first regular passenger and freight service between the ports of the Pacific Coast. Officials, clerics, and troops used his vessels exclusively. In the relations between Mexico and California he was the most influential person. Virmond was a fine type of man, an accomplished musician, an indefatigable collector of natural objects, and withal a most charitable person, always ready to assist his fellowmen, whether Germans, Americans, or Mexicans. His singular character we may surmise from the type of his employees, who were much more than ordinary clerks. Friedrich Becher, his one time associate, played an important role in California politics and society, was an expert equestrian, and a tireless perpetrator of practical jokes. Virmond's principal representative in California, Ferdinand Deppe, was a popular figure in the country and apparently more of a naturalist than a merchant. In 1836 he returned to Germany and worked as a botanist in the Royal Gardens of Potsdam. Another of Virmond's clerks, Eduard Vischer, settled in the country. He was a well known artist, and in later years published the first picture book of California.

In 1826 the land route from the United States to California was opened up by the first party of trappers under the leadership of Jedediah Smith. There were apparently no Germans in this party, but it was Heinrich Virmond whose generosity saved the trappers when they reached San Francisco in a deplorable condition. In Pattie's famous company, which crossed the plains at about the same time, was a "Dutchman," a live wire who by his "sweetness of temper, that was never ruffled and a calmness and patience that appeared proof against all events" did much to relieve the melancholy of his companions.

In 1831 two German-American trappers who were to play leading roles in the subsequent history of the country reached California soil: Jacob Primer Leese and William Wolfskill.

Leese was the son and on his mother's side the grandson of soldiers in the War of Independence. His father had left Germany to join LaFayette's expedition force. Wounded at the battle of Brandywine, he was carried from the field by his comrade and countryman, Adam Primer, whose daughter he later married. Their son Jacob, born in 1809 in Ohio, was destined to become the founder of modern San Francisco.

Wolfskill was a Kentuckian of German extraction whose ancestor had been, according to one authority, a favorite soldier of Frederick the Great. He had first been a Santa Fe trader, and in 1831, jointly with Ewing Young, he led a party of trappers over a new route to Southern California. This, known as the old Spanish Trail, became in later years the trading route between Santa Fe and Los Angeles.

The Coming of John August Sutter

With the secularization of church property in 1834 the first period of California history came to an end. The missions, deprived of their power, declined rapidly, and a comparative prosperity gave way to a desolate state of affairs. A new civilization was ushered in by the coming of a man who was to become the greatest of all California pioneers, and whose historical significance can hardly be overestimated: Johann August Sutter.

Sutter was born in 1803 in Kandern in Baden, and received his education in his native town. As a young man he went to Switzerland, and, failing in business, he emigrated in 1834 to New York. In the following years we find him as a Santa Fe trader, and in 1838 he decided to seek his fortune in California. By way of Oregon, Hawaii, and Alaska, Sutter finally reached the land of promise in 1839. For the next ten years the history of the Golden State is almost identical with the history of Sutter and his establishment.

Receiving permission from the governor to explore the Sacramento valley and to select a site for a settlement, Sutter established, with five white men and eight Kanakas whom he had brought from Hawaii, the colony of New Helvetia. The Sacramento valley, today one of the richest agricultural districts of the world, was at that time a hopeless wilderness inhabited by unruly Indians who had as yet had no contact with civilization. Sutter at once made his presence felt. His fair and tactful treatment of the Indians made them his friends, and with their help he became within a short time a veritable king in the Sacramento and Joaquin valleys. The virgin soil yielded a rich harvest, and Sutter's live-stock increased rapidly. A flour mill, a fishery, a vineyard, a distillery, a tannery, hunting and trapping expeditions, weaving of woolen blankets, making of hats, regular launch service to San Francisco,—no branch of agriculture or industry possible under the circumstances was left untried by Sutter. His colony was soon the nucleus of all economic activities in Northern California.

Sutter's Fort as it Appears Today

Within a year his position was so firmly established that he could threaten to declare the independence of California if the Mexicans should dare to interfere with his activities, and when in 1840 a number of Americans were expelled from the country by the Mexican government, they simply went to Sutter's Fort and were not further molested. The Mexican authorities recognized very early the influence of Sutter and deemed it best to be on a good footing with him. In 1841 he was formally invested with the wide tract between the Sacramento and Feather rivers, and at the same time he was made a justice and representative of the Mexican government in the North.

Nothing illustrates better the strong position of Sutter than the circumstance that the Russian government sold its possessions at Fort Ross and Bodega to the potentate of the Sacramento Valley when the Russian California colony was abandoned,—this in spite of the fact that Sutter was unable to pay down a single cent on the agreed purchasing price of $32,000. The acquisition of the Russian holdings greatly strengthened Sutter's position. He transferred the strong armament of Fort Ross to New Helvetia, created a regular little army, and made his fortress well nigh impregnable. In John Gantt he found a trained military commander, in Charles W. Fluegge an able diplomat, and in A. Hoover (Huber) and Samuel Kyburz honest managers of the agricultural enterprises of his colony.

When in 1844 a revolt broke out against California's new governor, Micheltorena, Sutter marched south with an army of 400 men, commanded by Gantt. He arrived, however. too late to save the day for the unlucky governor, who had just signed over to Sutter a new grant of 22 leagues. twice the amount which he already possessed. Although Sutter was arrested on his arrival, the authorities did not dare to remain on bad terms with so powerful a man. On the contrary, the new governor confirmed Sutters position as military commander of the northern frontier and as executive judge.

Sutter's charming personality, his buoyant optimism, his never failing generosity, have been attested by all who came in contact with him. He had the bearings and manners of an aristocrat of the old school, but was nevertheless a fine example of a democrat. His great success had not made him haughty and egotistic. Everyone received the same treatment, whether a high American or Mexican official or a poor emigrant or despised Indian.

As Sutter's greatest contribution to the history of the American West we must consider the fact that he started directly and indirectly the emigration to California which led to the opening up of the wide stretch of land between the Pacific and the Rocky Mountains. The intelligence of his unbelievable success spread rapidly, and by his numerous letters and reports published in the United States and in Europe Sutter inaugurated the great westward movement which alone made possible the marvellous development of the Far West.

In 1841 the first organized party of emigrants arrived at Fort Sutter. It consisted to a large extent of Germans, the most prominent among whom was Charles M. Weber, in honor of whom a river, a lake, and a county in Utah were named. From then on emigrant parties for California were organized in ever increasing numbers. Whether they came directly over the Sierras or by way of Oregon, it was always the magnetic power of Fort Sutter which attracted them. They knew that they would receive hearty welcome from the great pioneer, that their goods would be bought or exchanged, that Sutter would guarantee their character to the government, that families would be advised where to settle, and unattached men and women find temporary or permanent employment, whether Sutter needed them or not. To quote the words of W. F. Swasey, a fellow pioneer, "Sutter's Fort was the nucleus about which centered many of the remarkable characters who were destined to become founders of the State of California. It would require volumes to recite the numerous acts of kindness and hospitality so generously and eagerly extended by Captain Sutter to the poor, wearied, half-famished, and ill-clad imigrants. Food, clothing, and shelter were freely given without limit. Relief was despatched to the almost impenetrable fastnesses of the mountains, bearing succor, comfort, and joy to the helpless and despairing hearts of the snow-imprisoned travelers." This is not the isolated praise of a man who might have received special favors, but it is representative of all contemporary accounts of this great man. Helplessly the Mexican government looked on when Americans and Europeans began to flood the country. But there was no possibility of stopping the stream as long as Fort Sutter controlled the passes of the Sierras.

The best known of the early emigrant parties was the Donner party, whose tragic fate stands to the present day as a symbol of the sufferings and hardships of the early emigrants. The two Donner families came of German revolutionary stock and had been pioneer settlers in Sangamin County in Illinois, whence they started in the spring of 1846. The whole party consisted of ninety persons, largely Americans, Germans and Irish, with Jacob Donner as captain. By a series of misfortunes the march of the company had been delayed, and they became snow-bound in the high Sierras. They were obliged to camp near the present Donner Lake, where two years before a German-American lad, Moses Schallenberger, had for four winter months lived the life of a Robinson Crusoe. The entire party would probably have perished had not Sutter, with his usual generosity, despatched a train of mules laden with provisions. But neither Sutter's timely assistance nor the subsequent relief parties which started from New Helvetia could prevent half of the emigrants from perishing, the rest saving their lives only by eating the bodies of their dead comrades. A beautiful bronze monument, erected by the Native Sons and Daughters of the Golden West, marks the spot where occurred the worst disaster in Western American history.

The American Conquest

While Sutter had prepared the ground for the American occupation of California, the name of the famous Franco-American pioneer, John F. Fremont, is connected with the movement which led to the annexation of California. In 1842 Col. J. J. Abert, chief of the Corps of Topographical Engineers, sent Fremont out on his first expedition, which, however, did not reach the coast. There were several Germans in this party, and Fremont's right hand in this and his subsequent expeditions was Karl Preuss, a trained German engineer and topographer, upon whom should fall part of the honors showered upon Fremont. Preuss, who also drafted the first official map of California for the U. S. government, must be credited with the scientific results of Fremont's expeditions.

The second of Fremont's parties reached California, but might have come to a disastrous end had not Sutter sent out a relief party to save its members. The third expedition in 1845 was likewise only able to finish its work after Sutter had reprovisioned the party. When Fremont visited New Helvetia in December, 1845, he was royally received and entertained.

In March, 1846, the Mexicans, realizing the danger of Fremont's continued presence in California, decided to expel him from the country and surrounded his camp in the Salinas valley. Charles M. Weber, already a prominent man in San Jose, called together the settlers of his district to relieve Fremont's precarious situation. John Daubenbiss, a Bavarian, was sent north to arouse the settlers. Fremont, however, was able to escape unmolested and continued his march to Oregon. In the meantime the U. S. government, expecting the outbreak of the war, had decided to give Fremont free hand in California to forestall the designs of France and England upon the country. One of the two messengers sent by the American consul to recall Fremont was Samuel

Neal, a Holsteiner, who received for his services a land grant and became a well known pioneer stock breeder.

When Fremont returned and fostered the so-called Bear Flag Revolt, Sutter's situation became most embarrassing. His protection of American emigrants and his relations to Consul Larkin offer sufficient proof that Sutter was a friend of the United States, but, being a high Mexican official and having guaranteed the good behavior of many of the settlers who now revolted against the government, he resented the illegal procedure of Fremont, who appointed Lieutenant Kern Commander of the Fort and had several prominent pioneers arrested and interned in Sutter's stronghold. When, however, the war broke out, Sutter placed himself unreservedly on the side of the American republic, and on the eleventh of July, 1846, the Stars and Stripes were hoisted at New Helvetia.

The German element enlisted whole-heartedly in the war, and their pro rata number of active participants exceeded, as usual, all other nationalities. There was, however, little chance of attaining honors on the battlefield. There was no doubt about the outcome of the struggle, and no major engagements were fought on California soil. Captain Charles M. Weber distinguished himself in the campaign, and his mill in San Jose was the only one on the coast from which the army obtained flour. It is interesting to note that Charles Nordhoff, a Westphalian, who in later years made California famous by his books, paid his first visit to California during the war as sailor of the U. S. S. Columbus. Especially large was the number of Germans and German-Americans in Stevenson's New York Volunteers, many of whom became prominent California pioneers.

The topographers, surveyors, and draftsmen of the exploring and surveying parties sent out by the U. S. government subsequent to the conquest of California were in many cases Germans or Americans of German descent. D. Ottinger of the U. S. Revenue Service discovered and christened Humboldt Bay in the northern part of the State in 1850, and Arthur Schott of Stuttgart was a member of the commission to measure the new U. S.-Mexican boundary. The topographer and artist of the railroad survey along the 35th parallel, and of the expedition which measured and explored the Colorado River, was the well known German novelist, Balduin von Moellhausen.

Other Germans gained recognition in the pacifica-

tion of the Indians. Major S. P. Heintzelman, who commanded in Southern California from 1850 to 1855, made the southern route safe by establishing Fort Yuma. His services in dealing with the Indians earned him the high praise of his superior: "The General commanding congratulates you, and the officers of your command, on the termination of the Indian War in the South. To your good judgment, and untiring energy and perseverance, the country is under many obligations." In the northern district Andrew Snider, a Wurttemberger, became well known for his tactful handling of the Indians. He was made Agent of the Klammath Indian reservation, which under his guidance became the best in the state and a model for other reservations.

The Discovery of Gold

Upon the heels of the conquest of California followed another event, which changed the history of the West and the economic consequences of which had a profound influence upon the political conditions of Europe: the discovery of gold. In 1847 Sutter decided to build a saw mill at Coloma and put his head carpenter, James Marshall, in charge. On the 28th of January, 1848, Marshall and a German millwright in Sutter's employ, Peter Wimmer, discovered the first nugget of the precious metal in the race of the mill, and Mrs. Wimmer proved it to be gold by boiling it in her wash-kettle. The news of the discovery spread rapidly, and Benjamin P. Kooser, a Pennsylvania German and pioneer printer in San Francisco, acquainted the world with the discovery by his letters to the N. Y. Herald. A number of guide books were at once published in Germany. One of them, B. Schmoelder's *Wegweiser*, was translated into into English and exerted considerable influence upon the coming of the Argonauts. The German gold seekers, moderate and industrious, formed a large percentage of these and established a number of mining camps, among which were Stoutenburg, Mosquito Gulch, and Dutch Flat. Friedrich Gerstaecker, the writer, worked several months in the mines and wrote his interesting accounts and novels. Heinrich Schliemann, the greatest explorer of ancient Greece, was in 1850 a resident of San Francisco and became a U. S. citizen, while Hermann Ehrenberg, Arizona's great pioneer, discovered Gold Bluff and the mouth of the Klammath and drafted the first map of that region.

The finding of gold spelled the ruin of California's foremost pioneer, John August Sutter. He had hoped in vain to keep the discovery secret till the Sobrante grant of Micheltorena had been confirmed. With the gradual growth of the gold fever his employees left for the gold fields, the leather in the tannery spoiled, the wheat could not be harvested, his cattle were stolen, and his land appropriated by squatters. Authorities and law-abiding citizens were on his side, and regular battles were fought between the lawless element and the police. Yet the former were too numerous to be subdued, and Sutter had to await the decision of the courts. The Land Commission appointed by the U. S. Congress to settle the California claims found no flaw in the title of the Sobrante grant, and the District Court of Northern California concurred with the decision of the Commission. In 1864, however, the U. S. Supreme Court gave recognition to the appeal of the squatters and denied Sutter's claim on the technical ground that Micheltorena had signed the grant after he had been obliged to leave the capital. This meant Sutter's ruin. He had given away many titles on the Sobrante grant and had to make these good by granting new titles on his Alvarado grant, which the Supreme Court had confirmed. His heavy debt, which he could easily have paid off in a few years of calm development, became now a source of endless trouble. Unscrupulous lawyers did the rest. He could not even hold his beautiful Hock Farm, where he had intended to spend the rest of his life; and when his house was burned down by an incendiary, he left the state in bitterness. In 1880 he died in Lititz in Pennsylvania without having received restitution for the wrong done him.

Sutter's work has always received high praise and recognition. After the annexation of California he had been appointed Indian Agent of his district, discharging his new duties to the satisfaction of the government. In 1849 he was elected to the constituent assembly and acted for some time as its president. In 1853 the California legislature appointed him Major General, and military men presented him with a sword of honor. In 1855 the legislature purchased a life size oil painting of Sutter to adorn the capitol, and ten years later it voted a monthly pension of $250 for him, which was paid for ten years. On the occasion of his death General Sherman, General Fremont, and many other prominent men paid the highest tribute to Sutter's character and

17

his work, and the resolution of the Associated Pioneers of territorial days in California contained the following passage: "To General Sutter more than to any other actor in the events which made California a part of our national domain, is due the permanent acquisition of that rich and beautiful region of our country."

Los Angeles and San Francisco

While the pioneer history of California in a narrower sense is mainly the history of San Francisco Bay and of the Sacramento and San Joaquin valleys, Southern California experienced a much earlier development in pastoral California. Los Angeles was an important centre, with a liberal sprinkling of Germans among its inhabitants, before San Francisco or Sacramento came into existence. The first German to settle in Los Angeles and one of the first foreign settlers of the country was Johann Groeningen. He was one of the three sailors saved from the wreck of the *Danube* in 1826. He took a prominent part in the development of early Los Angeles and was a popular figure in the South, being known as Juan Cojo because he limped. His cane is preserved in the county museum. A few years later Jacob P. Leese opened a store in the southern metropolis, followed in 1832 by J. D. Meyer, the first blacksmith, and in 1835 by Nicholas Fink, the first shoemaker of Los Angeles.

In the fifties two German engineers, Georg Hansen and Franz Lecouvreur, surveyed and laid out the larger part of the modern city of Los Angeles. To the foresight of the former the city owes the Elysian Park. Concerning the part played by Germans in commercial cultural, and political Los Angeles we find detailed information in H. Newmark's book, *Sixty years in Southern California*, an excellent historical account and a fine human document. Newmark, a German Jew, was a pioneer merchant who lived to see the city grow from a little town to the largest city on the coast. From him we learn that most of the early artisans were Germans, and that the Teuton element played likewise a prominent part in politics. Many of the city and county offices were filled by Germans, and the first political parade in 1854 was organized by three Germans. Los Angeles, today famous for its flower gardens, was like most pioneer settlements a bleak town until Henry Schaeffer, the first gunsmith of Los Angeles, surrounded his house with flowers.

Celebration of the Fourth of July at Leese's House.

Celebration of the Fourth of July at Leese's House

A trader from the southern city, Jacob P. Leese, must be credited with being the founder of modern San Francisco. Governor Chico rewarded the services of this German-American pioneer by granting him in 1836 a hundred yard lot anywhere on the shores of San Francisco Bay to establish a trading post. Little did Leese realize that the spot which he selected would be within a couple of decades the metropolis of the Pacific Ocean. His choice fell upon the beach of the Yerba Buena cove at the northwest corner of the San Francisco peninsula. His house was completed on the fourth of July, 1836. On that day the American flag was hoisted for the first time on California soil, and in his house the first celebration of the glorious Fourth was held, which owing to the non-existence of the Volstead act, ended on the evening of the fifth. This house and the store opened by Leese and two partners formed the nucleus of the town of Yerba Buena, later changed to San Francisco. It gradually spread over the northern end of the peninsula and absorbed the two Spanish pueblos at the mission and the presidio. In 1837 Leese married the sister of a fellow pioneer, General Vallejo, and their child, Rosalie, was the first American child born in San Francisco.

Until the time of the gold rush the growth of the city was rather slow. In 1845 there were only a few hundred inhabitants, the German being the chief element beside the natives and Americans. The first blacksmith, tailor, baker, and butcher, and many of the early traders, were Germans. Some of these pioneers, Emanuel Russ, James Lick, and Adolph Sutro, deserve special mention.

Emanuel Russ, a native of beautiful Thuringia and a descendent of a noble Polish family, came to New York in 1832 and established himself as a jeweler. By 1845 Russ had accumulated a considerable fortune. While attending the funeral obesquies of President Jackson his store was robbed and his large family reduced to poverty. Undismayed, he and his older sons enlisted as privates in the New York Volunteers, a regiment bound for the seat of war in California. Arriving in 1847, Russ obtained the lumber of the ship's bunk and erected a house for his family at the site on which in later years the well known Russ House stood, and which is today occupied by the Russ Building, the largest structure west of Chicago. Within two years Russ had become the largest real estate owner in San Francisco. The famous Russ Garden, established in 1852, was for many years the only suburban resort where the German May-Day, the Fourth of July, and other festivities were held. Russ and his descendents attained great prominence in the commercial and political life of their adopted city.

James Lick was a Pennsylvania German who landed in California in 1848 after an eventful career. Already a well-to-do man, he invested his money in apparently worthless sand dunes, which in due time made him enormously wealthy. He was rather unsociable and whimsical, and proved his queerness by having his flour mill in San Jose finished in mahogany. The wealth and variety of California in trees and shrubs is largely due to Lick, who imported them from all parts of the world. During his lifetime counted as a miser he bequeathed his large fortune to charitable and scientific enterprises, the largest sum providing for the erection of the world famous Lick Observatory, now the property of the state university.

Of an entirely different stamp was Adolph Sutro, a Rhinelander. Arriving in San Francisco in 1850, he was for ten years a small merchant until he became interested in the Comstock mine in Nevada, originally discovered by two Germans from Pennsylvania, the Grosch brothers. He decided to build a tunnel for draining and ventilation. When the big money interests tried to prevent the completion of the project, he fought a battle which for virulence and persistency has had no equal on the Pacific Coast. His pluck and courage won the day, and he completed the 7000 yard long tunnel at the cost of $6,500,000. Later he led the fight against the Funding Bill of the Central Pacific Railroad and saved the people many millions. His struggle for civic betterment was recognized when he was elected mayor of San Francisco. It was also Sutro who introduced Bermuda and Bent grasses, by which many acres of dunes were reclaimed. Sutro Heights, the Cliff House, Sutro Forest, and Sutro Baths, bear witness to the generosity of this great German-Californian.

A pioneer of the medical profession in San Francisco was Frederick Zeile, a Wurttemberger. Detained in Panama in 1849, he won the title of public benefactor for his unselfish services and successfully urged the local authorities to build a hospital for the emigrants. In San Francisco he established the first public hospital on the coast, and to his efforts was mainly due the gradual spread of the bath tub and the public bath in San Francisco.

The military leader of the Germans in early San Francisco was Col. Fred G. E. Tittel. He had come west during the Mexican war as a member of the third U. S. Artillery and was later an officer in the state militia. During the days of the Vigilantes he was captain of the Fusileers, mostly Germans, and at the outbreak of the civil war he became colonel of the German Regiment whose prompt action helped to save California for the Union.

Charles Kohler was one of the original incorporators of the San Francisco cable road system, and in 1857 A. W. von Schmidt, with two partners, started the San Francisco water works and gave the city its first regular water supply. Albert Miller in 1854 established the first savings bank, and John Eckfeldt was the first coiner of the U. S. Mint, erected the same year. Two German institutions dating from pioneer days gained wide recognition as semi-public institutions,—the German Benevolent Society and the German Loan Association, "to whose capital, borrowed at very reasonable rates of interest, much is due for the industrial development of the country"—(Bancroft).

City Building and Industries

San Francisco's claim to predominance did not remain unchallenged. The first to conceive the idea of locating the metropolis at some other place on the shores of the Bay was Captain B. Schmoelder, who did much to promote German immigration. In 1847 he started a trading company and intended to found a German city on the northern shore of San Francisco Bay. The outbreak of the gold rush killed the project. It was, however, again taken up by Dr. Robert Semple, who showed his distrust in San Francisco's future by giving away his valuable city lot and investing his money in the town of Benicia. One of his German associates E. H. von Pfister, started the town by opening a store. But in spite of the favorable location Benicia soon lost the race with her older sister.

In the building of the pioneer cities the Germans have everywhere played an important part. From the ferry hut of Nicolaus Altgeier sprang the little town, Nicolaus, on the Sacramento river. Bloomfield in Sonma was named after F. G. Blume, a pioneer physician who settled in 1847. The first store in San Jose was opened by Charles M. Weber in 1842, and Jacob D. Hoppe, an early newspaperman and member of the constituent assembly, was one of the projectors of Halo Chemuck, another town killed by the gold fever. The first to realize the value of California's springs was Andreas Hoeppner, a German who had long been in the Russian Alaska service. In 1847 he founded the watering place of Annenthal in Sonoma, where General Sherman was one of his first guests. Hoeppner, who was an accomplished artist and musician, was a popular figure in early California and gained quite a reputation by defeating the Swiss pioneer, Vioget, in an eating match.

Most striking evidence of the importance of the German element in the Golden State is the fact that the three pioneer towns of the interior valley, Stockton, Sacramento, and Marysville, were all founded by Germans.

Charles N. Weber, was, next to Sutter, the most notable German pioneer during the transition period of California history. He was born in Hamburg in 1814, and in 1836 came to New Orleans and took part in the Texan war. In 1841 he crossed the plains with the first immigrant train, was for some time in the employ of Sutter, and then a pioneer merchant of San Jose. In 1845 he started the town, Tuleburg, on the San Joaquin river, which he later named Stockton. Favorably located, Stockton became the centre for the Southern gold fields. In 1851 Weber deeded all streets, channels, and squares to the city. Honored as one of the greatest pioneers of the country, he died in 1881.

Stockton in 1849

In the same year in which Weber founded his settlement Sutter laid out the town, Sutterville. Believing rightly that the low land around his fort was not favorable to a large city, he selected a spot three miles down the river on high ground. Nevertheless the town around Fort Sutter had, with its ferry and stores, too good a start over its rival, and Sutter had finally to give in. Against his better judgment, which was proven by the devastating floods of later years, Sutter charged his son with laying out the city of Sacramento. Here the first brick house ever built in California was erected by Georg Zinns, an Alsatian.

The present city of Marysville grew out of the settlement of Theodor Cordua, originally called after his native land, New Mecklenburg.

Hand in hand with the founding of cities went the development of industries. Not only were the Germans the first craftsmen in many cities, they also started many of the important industries of the state. The first tannery outside the one at Fort Ross was opened by Sutter in 1843. Georg Zinns in 1847 started the first brick-kiln in Suttersville, turning out 40,000 bricks the first year. Hagler's mill in Sonoma was probably the first in the state, being erected about the same time as Weber's in San Jose. The first carriage factory was established by a German in Los Angeles, and the first salt works started by Weber in Alameda. The abundance of tallow led early to the manufacturing of soap. Two Germans, J. J. Bergin in San Francisco and J. H. Heilmann in Sacramento, established the first factories in 1850. Brewing beer and making of wine were, of course, from the very beginning in the hands of Germans. The first important brewery in San Francisco was opened by J. Wieland, whose "deep, strong, and warm-hearted nature," as Bancroft observes, "had gained him the hearts of the community." Charles Kohler and J. Frohling, started wine making on a large scale and gave a strong impulse to California's viniculture. The first macaroni factory was started by a German and an Italian, and the first weaving mill and the first shoe factory owed their origin likewise to Germans. Julius Bandmann introduced Nobel's explosives and was the first to manufacture powder and dynamite on the coast, while one Adelsdorfer introduced Swedish matches. Needless to say that the early manufacture of musical instruments and billiard tables was also in the hands of Germans.

Agriculture and Colonization

With the secularization of the misions the primitive agriculture introduced by the padres rapidly declined, and was revived, not by the native Californians, but by the American, German, and French settlers.

The first vineyard in the country was planted by William Lobe in Los Angeles as early as 1831. Grape growing on a large scale was begun by Charles Kohler and John Frohling, who gave up their musical profession in 1852 and started raising grapes in Los Angeles County. Since that time the Germans have almost exclusively been the pioneer vineyardists in all parts of the state.

William Wolfskill, a German-Kentuckian, was the pioneer of California's citriculture. In 1841 he planted an orange grove near Los Angeles, which was soon the largest in the United States. In 1862 Wolfskill is said to have still owned two thirds of all orange trees in the state, although at that time Leonard Rose had already started his famous orange grove, which for many years was a regular show-place of the country. Wolfskill's brother John was the first large fruit grower in Yolo county, while Dr. J. Strentzel, the father-in-law of the naturalist,

John Muir, became with his Alhambra orchard a pioneer fruit grower on San Francisco Bay. H. F. Teschemacher, later mayor of San Francisco, introduced the first almond seeds from the Mediteranean, and the culture of sugar beets is inseparably connected with the name of Claus Spreckels.

The first cattle raisers on a large scale in Southern California were William Wolfskill and Ludwig Phillips, while Samuel Neal, a Holsteiner, John Rohrer, an Al-satian, and Julian Neuschwander, a Swiss, were pioneer stockmen in the North. The most successful stockmen, however, were two Wurttembergers, Henry Miller and Charles Lux, who in the early fifties imported cattle from the East and from Europe and started wholesale live-stock raising. Thirty years later they owned 750,-000 acres of land, their horned cattle being estimated at 100,000 and their sheep at 80,000.

The dry season of California made irrigation a prerequisite of successful agriculture. The Canal and Reservoir Company which Georg Hansen organized in Los Angeles contributed much to the development of the south, and to Henry Miller, the cattleman, "is largely due the successful operation of the San Joaquin and Kings river canal company, the largest irrigation enterprise on the coast" (Bancroft). In later years Professor E. W. Hilgard, a son of a "Latin Farmer" of Belleville, Illinois, and for many years Dean of the College of Agriculture of the University of California, was active in promoting irrigation in California and Arizona.

The conditions of early California were well adapted to agriculture on a co-operative basis. Owing to the discovery of gold, all early experiments failed, however. Sutter was the first who attempted to establish in New Helvetia a German-Swiss colony, which soon took on an international aspect. In 1847 a number of Germans, all members of the New York Volunteers who had received land grants, formed a company to establish a settlement 150 miles south of San Francisco. With true German inclination the first act was to establish a German-English library. Beyond this stage the colony does not seem to have progressed, when the reports from the gold fields began to exert their magnetic power.

A few years later a number of educated Germans decided to seek a new home in California after the failure of the revolution of 1849. G. A. Bergenroth, an East Prussian, was sent to explore the ground with a view to founding a German settlement. Taken ill, robbed of his possessions, and unlucky in the mines, Bergenroth's report was so unfavorable that the idea was apparently given up. Bergenroth himself, without funds for the return trip, became a hunter and with a group of nondescript fellows formed twenty miles south of San Francisco a kind of colony, "wielding a dictatorial authority over these anything but amenable subjects by the sheer vigor of his resolution and the superiority of his physical strength." It was in this strange community that the first vigilance committee of Northern California came into existence.

It was not until 1857 that the first successful co-operative colony was established in California. Fifty Germans from San Francisco bought a tract of 1165 acres about thirty miles from Los Angeles at two dollars per acre. The company consisted mainly of mechanics and artisans, with a sprinkling of teachers and musicians, and had also a poet in their ranks, as was to be expected among half a hundred Germans at that period. This colony is an excellent example of what co-operation can do. Georg Hansen, the pioneer engineer of Los Angeles, was charged with the temporary management of the settlement. City lots and farms were parcelled out and planted. The different members worked in San Francisco until the vineyards and orchards became productive. Then the homesteads were distributed by lot. Those receiving a more valuable piece of land had to pay the difference into the common treasury, out of which were compensated those to whose lot had fallen a less valuable share. After this had been done, co-operation ceased. The colony receiving the name Anaheim proved to be a great success, and the many colonies formed in later years around Los Angeles were modeled after this German pioneer settlement, which, according to the historian Cleland, "for many years was almost a synonym for prosperity and industry throughout the South."

OFFICERS

PRESIDENT—CARL E. SCHMIDT, Oscoda, Mich.
1st VICE PRESIDENT—PROF. A. B. FAUST, Ithaca, N. Y.
2nd VICE PRESIDENT—DR. OTTO L. SCHMIDT, Chicago, Ill.
3rd VICE PRESIDENT—PROF. RICHARD C. SCHIEDT,
Lancaster, Pa.
4th VICE PRESIDENT—DR. L. A. FRITSCHE, New Ulm, Minn.
5th VICE PRESIDENT—DR. C. S. LEEDE, Seattle, Wash.
TREASURER—DR. ROBERT ROESSLER, Hoboken, N. J.
FINANCIAL SEC'Y.—FRED C. GARTNER, 505 Finance Bldg.,
Philadelphia, Pa.
CORRESPONDING SEC'Y.—DR. CARL SELMER, 27 Parkhurst St., Newark, N. J.

MEMBERSHIP REFEREE

Hon. E. K. Vietor, Southern District.
Col. Fred E. Shubel, North Western District
Hon. C. H. Becker, Western District.
Carl F. W. Ellinger, Northern District.
Otto A. Stiefel, Eastern District.

HONORARY MEMBERS

Hon. J. F. Minturn, Supreme Court of New Jersey.
Hon. T. St. J. Gaffney, Summit, N. J.
Prof. Harry Elmer Barnes, Smith College, Mass
Senator Robert L. Owen, Oklahoma.
Prof. Dr. John Russell, University of Detroit.
Prof. Dr. H. Harris Aall, University of Oslo.

FINANCE COMMITTEE

Emil Stohn, Jersey City, N. J.
Rud. Pagenstecher, New York City.
Godfrey Schirmer, Denver. Col.
Carl August Stern, New York City.
Henry C. Steneck, Hoboken, N. J.

HISTORICAL COMMITTEE

Hon. Emil Baensch, Manitowoc, Wis.; Prof. Dr. F. Bauer, Elm-
hurst, Ill.; Prof. Dr. J. V. Breitwieser, Berkeley, Cal.; Prof. Dr.
John Eiselmeier, Milwaukee, Wis.; Prof. Dr. B. Faust, Ithaca,
N. Y.; Prof. Dr. Max Griebsch, Madison, Wis.; Prof. Dr. E. G.
Gudde, Berkeley, Cal.; Oscar F. Keydel, Detroit, Mich.; Hon. Max
Otto von Klock, Boston, Mass.; Rev. Carl Kretzmann, Orange,
N. J.; H. J. A. Lacher, Waukesha, Wis.; V. W. Richter, Chicago,
Ill.; Victor F. Ridder, New York City; Harry Rickel, Mount
Clemens, Mich.; Prof. Rich C. Schiedt, Lancaster, Pa.; Prof. Wm.
Schmidt, St. Paul, Minn.; Louis Schnitzer, New York City; Fred
F. Schrader, Chicago, Ill.; Prof. Dr. Martin Schuetze, Chicago,
Ill.; Dr. Carl Selmer, Newark, N. J.; Geo. Sylvester Vierreck,
New York City.

Historical Publications of The Concord Society of America

Oct. 6, 1912

German Address before the Germantown Delegation of Germantown, Pa., at Mt. Vernon, Va., delivered by Dr. R. Roessler, N. J.

Oct. 6, 1915

Dr. C. J. Hexamer, by Conrad Nies

Oct. 6, 1916

The Prayer of a German-American, by Carl Castelhun, Cal.

Oct. 6, 1917

"Walhalla," dedicated to Mr. Carl E. Schmidt, Walhalla, Oscoda, Mich.. by Dr. R. Roessler.

Oct. 6, 1918

The Prayer of a German Swiss, by Gottlieb Graber, Wis.

Oct. 6, 1919

1683-1920. Former German-American Handbook, by F. F. Schrader.

Oct. 6, 1920

Doughboys on the Witness Stand, by Forrest and Robert Lenoux, Gonzales, La.

Oct. 6, 1921

Our Debt to France, by R. C. Dasher.

Historical Bulletin No. 1, 1922.

The Period from 1564-1682 incl., by Otto Lohr, 25c.

Historical Bulletin No. 2, 1923.

Prussia and the United States, by F. F. Schrader, N. Y., 25c.

Historical Bulletin No. 3, 1924.

General Washington's Bodyguards, by V. W. Richter, Ill., 25c.

Historical Bulletin No. .4, 1925.

Friedrich List, Whom American History Forgot, a Biographical Review, by Harry Rickel, Mich., 25c.

Historical Bulletin No. 5, 1925.

Striking Facts About the Germans in the United States, by Prof. A. B. Faust, Cornell University, N. Y., 25c.

Historical Bulletin No. 6, 1927.

German Pioneers in Early California, by Prof. E. G. Gudde, Berkeley, Cal., 25c.

Historical Bulletin No. 7, 1927.

The German John Adam Treutlen, The Revolutionary Martyr— Governor of Georgia (1733-1782) by Rev. Karl Kretzmann, Orange, N. J., 25c.

Historical Bulletin No. 8, 1927.

The Battle of Oriscany, Aug. 6, 1777, by Max Otto von Klock, Boston, Mass., 25c.

Historical Bulletin No. 9, 1927.

The German Coast of Louisiana, by Rev. Karl Kretzmann, Orange, N. J., 25c.

Historical Bulletin No. 10, 1927.

German American History, an Outline, by Dr. Carl Selmer, Hunter College, N. Y. C., 50c.

Address at the Annual Banquet of the Concord Society at the Waldorf Astoria, No. 1926, by Prof. R. C. Schiedt, Lancaster, Pa.

and

The German-Americans During the World War, by Hon. T. St. J. Gaffney, Summit, N. J. Honorary Member of the Concord Society, 25c.

IN PREPARATION

The Mecklenburg Declaration of Independence, Charlotte, N. C., May 20, 1775. From the viewpoint: Reflecting British War lies, their flat acceptance by official America and veiled Tory influence, by Dr. R. Roessler, 25c.

Supplementary of Bulletin No. 1, by Dr. C. Selmer, Hunter College, N. Y., 25c.

Annual Report and Speeches at the Meeting and Banquet in Chicago, on August 20th, 1927, 25c.

OTHER PUBLICATIONS

The German Element in the United States, by Prof. A. B. Faust, Published by the Steuben Society of America. $2.50.

The German Element in Wisconsin, by H. J. A. Lacher, published by Muehlenberg Unit No. 30 of the Steuben Society of America, Milwaukee, Wis., 25c.

The German Influence in the Making of Michigan, by John A. Russell, A. M. L. L. D., University of Detroit, Mich., $10.00.

A German American Boy, (First Martyr of the Revolution), by Hon. Emil Baensch, Manitovoc, Wis., 50c.

Das Deutschtum in Anglo-Amerika, by Prof. John Eiselmeier, Milwaukee, Wis., 25c.

The **Russian Imperial Conspiracy 1892-1914,** by Senator Robert
L. Owen, of Oklahoma, Honorary Member of the Concord
Society, $2.00.

The **Genesis of the World War,** by Prof. H. E. Barnes, North-
hampton, Mass., Honorary Member of the Concord Society,
$5.00.

Treason to American Tradition, by Chas. Grant Miller, 25c.

Send Orders to

DR. C. SELMER, Secretary, 27 Parkhurst St., Newark, N. J.

DR. ROBERT ROESSLER, Treasurer, 522 Hudson St., Hoboken,
N. J.

AMERICAN MONTHLY, 93 5th Ave., N. Y. City

CONCORDIA PUBLISHING HOUSE, 3558 S. Jefferson Ave.,
St. Louis, Mo.

**"MEMBERS RECEIVE ALL PUBLICATIONS OF THE
SOCIETY FREE."**

Other Books by the author:

<u>CD-ROMs:</u>
CD: German-American Biographical Index (Midwest Families)
CD: The German Immigrant in America
CD: Germany and America 1450-1700
CD: German Pioneer Life and Domestic Customs
CD: German Pioneer Lifestyle
CD: The German Colonial Era, (four volumes)
CD: Germans, Volume 2

<u>Books:</u>
Covington's German Heritage
The Pennsylvania Germans: James Owen Knauss, Jr.'s Social History
Dayton's German Heritage: Karl Karstaedt's Golden Jubilee History of
the German Pioneer Society of Dayton, Ohio
Kentucky's German Pioneers: H.A. Rattermann's History
Memories of the Battle of New Ulm: Personal Accounts of the Sioux
Uprising. L. A. Fritsche's History of Brown County, Minnesota (1916)
Outbreak and Massacre by the Dakota Indians in Minnesota in 1862:
Marion P. Satterlee's Minute Account of the Outbreak, with Exact
Locations, Names of All Victims, Prisoners at Camp Release, Refugees at
Fort Ridgely, etc. Complete List of Indians killed in battle and those hung,
and those pardoned at Rock Island, Iowa
German-American Achievements: 400 Years of Contributions to America
Ohio's German Heritage
Cincinnati's German Heritage
Louisiana's German Heritage: Louis Voss' Introductory History
Amana: William Rufus Perkins' and Barthinius L. Wick's History of the
Amana Society, or Community of True Inspiration
Early German-American Newspapers: Daniel Miller's History
German Americans in the Revolution
Biography of Baron von Steuben, The Army of the American Revolution
and its Organizer: Rudolf Cronau's Biography of Baron von Steuben
German-Americana: A Bibliography
Custer: Frederick Whittaker's Complete Life of General George A. Custer,
Major General of Volunteers, Brevet Major General U.S. Army and
Lieutenant-Colonel Seventh U.S. Cavalry
German Immigration to America: The First Wave

www.ingramcontent.com/pod-product-compliance
Lightning Source LLC
Chambersburg PA
CBHW060703280326
41933CB00012B/2280